APPLE

ABDO
Publishing Company

TECHNOLOGY
PIONEERS

APPLE

THE COMPANY AND ITS VISIONARY FOUNDER, STEVE JOBS

by Marcia Amidon Lusted

Content Consultant
Adel Elmaghraby
Director, Innovative and Emerging Technologies Lab,
J. B. Speed School of Engineering
University of Louisville

CREDITS

Published by ABDO Publishing Company, PO Box 398166, Minneapolis, MN 55439. Copyright © 2012 by Abdo Consulting Group, Inc. International copyrights reserved in all countries. No part of this book may be reproduced in any form without written permission from the publisher. The Essential Library™ is a trademark and logo of ABDO Publishing Company.

Printed in the United States of America,
North Mankato, Minnesota
122011
012012

 THIS BOOK CONTAINS AT LEAST 10% RECYCLED MATERIALS.

Editor: Melissa York
Copy Editor: Angela Wiechmann
Series design: Emily Love
Cover and interior production: Marie Tupy

Library of Congress Cataloging-in-Publication Data
Lusted, Marcia Amidon.
 Apple : the company and its visionary founder, Steve Jobs / by Marcia Amidon Lusted.
     p. cm. -- (Technology pioneers)
  ISBN 978-1-61783-331-1
 1. Apple Computer, Inc.--History--Juvenile literature. 2. Computer industry--United States--History--Juvenile literature. 3. Jobs, Steve, 1955-2011. 4. Businesspeople--United States--Biography--Juvenile literature. 5. Success in business--Juvenile literature. I. Title.
  HD9696.2.U64L87 2012
  338.7'610040973--dc23
                           2011045750

TABLE OF CONTENTS

Steve Jobs presents Apple's original iPad.

WHAT YOU NEED BEFORE YOU NEED IT

O n January 27, 2010, at a press conference at the Yerba Buena Center for the Arts in San Francisco, California, Apple Inc. CEO Steve Jobs held up a new device the company had created. It was a small, portable computing device called

the iPad, just a half inch (1.3 cm) thick, less than
one foot (0.3 m) in length, and weighing less than
two pounds (0.9 kg). As Jobs held up the device, he
called the tablet "a truly magical and revolutionary
product. What this device does is extraordinary. It is
the best browsing experience you've ever had. . . . It's
unbelievably great . . . way better than a laptop. Way
better than a smartphone."[1]

Jobs, a thin man wearing his usual blue jeans,
sneakers, and black turtleneck sweater, noted there
was a need for a device that would do certain
tasks better than either a laptop computer or a
smartphone. He explained the iPad was the first
in a third category of devices that would browse
the web, manage e-mail, provide
music, and read e-books better
than any other previous device.

A SMASH SUCCESS

Jobs pointed out that more than
75 million consumers already knew
how to use the iPad because they
were already using the iPod touch
for their music and the iPhone
to communicate with each other.
Millions more already had credit
card accounts with the iTunes
Store, which would enable them

Since its introduction, the iPad
has been a huge hit. Early on,
consumers lined up at Apple
retail stores in order to purchase one. As of June 2011,
Apple had sold 25 million
iPads, and between June and
October of that year, it sold 11
million more.

to purchase e-books, music, and apps for their iPads with just a few touches of the screen. Jobs summed up the iPad by saying, "Our most advanced technology in a magical and revolutionary device at an unbelievable price."[2]

Consumers would be able to use the iPad as a computer, read books and magazines on it, download applications from Apple, import photos, and watch movies and television shows—all using a touch screen. Once again, Jobs and the innovators at Apple had shown consumers what they needed before they even knew they needed it. And once again, people who liked to be the first ones to have new technology lined up at Apple stores around the country, hoping to be one of the first to own an iPad.

The iPad was just the newest achievement in a series of Apple inventions that had become part of everyday life in the United States and around the world. From Macs to iPods, iPhones, Apple TV, and then iPads, Apple had continually invented or improved upon its products until many people found themselves unable to imagine life without the devices. In a world increasingly focused on instant gratification and instant communication, the company always seemed to know just what the public needed and how to present it to them. As

Jobs said, "People don't know what they want until you show it to them."[3] And he seemed to have the ability to know exactly what those things were. Today, billions of Apple products, from the smallest iPod nano to the most sophisticated computer, are used all over the world.

STARTING SMALL AND STRUGGLING

Similar to most companies, Apple started small and was not an instant success. It was founded in 1976, during a time when very few people encountered computers on a daily basis. Apple was the dream of two young men, Steve Jobs and Steve Wozniak, who had

THE FIRST COMPUTERS

It is hard to believe today that small home computers have not always been available to consumers. When Apple was first founded in 1976, most computers were huge, bulky things that often occupied entire rooms in order to have as much computing power as today's most basic cell phone. The oldest computers, such as the 1951 UNIVAC computer (the first commercial model) used vacuum tubes and relied on punch cards to convey programming instructions. Eventually computers began using transistors instead of vacuum tubes, which made them smaller but still bulky. Most computers were a collection of parts manufactured by different companies, and they usually required more than one person to operate them. The idea of a personal computer in every home, let alone one that could be carried around, seemed as unrealistic as flying cars or teleportation. The first microprocessor chip was invented in 1971, which made small personal computers possible. The first real home computer was the Altair in 1974. But, it would be decades before home computers became affordable for most people, not just for hobbyists and institutions.

a shared fascination with computers and wanted to try building their own. Eventually they would build computers that were accessible to regular people, unlike the huge, expensive models only wealthy people or large institutions such as universities could afford. But the launch of the personal computer did not go smoothly. It would take years of trying new ideas and sometimes failing before Apple would become the success it is today.

"Our first computers were born not out of greed or ego but in the revolutionary spirit of helping common people rise above the most powerful institutions."[4]

—*Steve Wozniak*

THE FACE OF APPLE

Jobs was the face of Apple, the man who always stood on a stage, announcing another new Apple product to the world. Wozniak was no longer employed full-time by the company as of 1985, although he remained a shareholder. Jobs's vision, both in product development and in marketing, was largely responsible for the company's success. It was not always a smooth ride for Jobs and the company he helped start. He himself was not an easy man to work with, and he actually was forced to leave Apple earlier in its history when the company was struggling to survive. But Jobs's persistence, and his ability to create ideas and market them successfully, ultimately led him back to Apple and made it the largest technology company in the world.

In March 2011, Jobs made one of his last appearances at the launch of the iPad 2. He surprised the audience by appearing on stage even though he was taking medical leave from the company. As usual, Jobs's ability to make every new-product presentation seem like something life changing and amazing made the release an event rather than a marketing strategy.

Seven months later, the man who had been such a force behind

NATIONAL MEDAL OF TECHNOLOGY

On February 19, 1985, Steve Jobs and Steve Wozniak were jointly awarded the National Medal of Technology by President Ronald Reagan. They received the honor, which is given only to the country's leading innovators, for their achievements with Apple Computer.

Apple died. As people around the world paid tribute to Jobs and the part he played in Apple, they looked back at how such a major company got its start in a suburban garage in Cupertino, California, just 35 years earlier. +

An Apple fan pays tribute to Jobs on his iPhone.

Steve Jobs did not fit in well in high school.

STEVE JOBS

lthough Apple owes its start to both Steve Jobs and Steve Wozniak, it was Jobs who played the bigger role throughout the company's history and whose personality and powers of persuasion helped achieve his goals. But Jobs's childhood was not one of stellar achievement and success. He was a regular kid who had a knack for tinkering with things, a different way of thinking, and an extroverted personality that made him unafraid of asking for what he wanted.

EARLY DAYS

Steven Paul Jobs was born in San Francisco, California, on February 24, 1955. His mother, at the time an unmarried graduate student, put him up for adoption. It wasn't until Jobs was a grown man and famous that he discovered who his parents were: Joanne Schieble and Abdulfattah "John" Jandali, who had come to the United States from Syria as a graduate student. Just weeks after his birth, his mother, known at that time only as "Jane Doe," signed him over to Paul and Clara Jobs, a married couple living in San Francisco. They had been trying to have a child for ten years before they adopted Steve.

Paul Jobs was good with his hands and good at tinkering with

MONA SIMPSON

Jobs later discovered that he had a full sister, born to his biological parents after they married. Her name is Mona Simpson, and although she grew up in Los Angeles, California, she and Jobs did not know of each other's existence. As adults, they became close. Jobs said, "We're family. She's one of my best friends in the world."[1]

cars, which he would buy, fix up, and resell at a profit. He had never attended college, but he served in the Coast Guard during World War II (1939– 1945), and he later earned money by repossessing cars for a finance company. He sold real estate for a time, but ultimately worked as a machinist. Jobs's mother, Clara, worked part-time as a payroll clerk while raising Steve and later his sister, Patty.

As a kid, Steve needed constant supervision because of his endless curiosity. At one point, he burned his hand by jamming a bobby pin into an electric outlet to see what would happen. Another time he had to be rushed to the hospital after tasting a bottle of ant poison just to see what it was like. But he was also a regular kid in many ways, playing roles in his neighbor's home movies, riding his bike, and watching television.

However, Steve did not get along with other kids once he started school, a pattern that would continue through most of high school. A schoolmate later described him as a "loner, pretty much of a crybaby. He didn't quite fit in with everyone else. He wasn't one of the guys."[2] Instead of hanging out with other kids, Steve often wandered around his neighborhood and visited the workshops of some of his adult neighbors, learning about their projects and how to put things together. School became worse when Steve attended junior high at Crittenden Middle School, which was known for discipline problems and troublemakers. Steve already had a reputation for pulling pranks that often got him in trouble and led to suspensions. He refused to do assignments he felt were a waste of time. Jobs himself later said, "I was pretty bored in school, and I turned into a little terror."[3]

Ultimately, Steve refused to return to Crittenden the following year, and his parents, already worried he would become a juvenile delinquent, agreed. The family moved to Los Altos to get into a different school district. There, Steve found himself living near scientists who were working for businesses making new technological advances, such as defense and technology company Lockheed. The city was the center of a region that would soon become known as Silicon Valley, a hotbed of technological innovation.

SILICON VALLEY

Silicon Valley is a nickname for an area of California located in the southern San Francisco Bay region. When Jobs and Wozniak were growing up, the area was just beginning to get its reputation as home to companies that produced the silicon microchips needed by the computer industry. The area also attracted investors who wanted to put money into the new and growing technology industry. The region is still considered a center for high-tech research and development companies.

HIGH SCHOOL AND BEYOND

At Cupertino Junior High and then at Homestead High in Los Altos, Jobs began making friends with other kids who had the same interest in electronics he did. One of Jobs's friends, Bill Fernandez, lived across the street from the Wozniak family. Father Jerry Wozniak was an engineer with Lockheed, and he was a mentor to Fernandez in the area of electronics. His son, Steve Wozniak, was five years older than Bill. The younger Wozniak helped Fernandez out with science projects from time to time.

During the summer of 1969, when Wozniak was already in college, he and a friend designed a computer they hoped to build themselves. When the friend left to attend college, Wozniak persuaded Fernandez to help him. They built what they called the "Cream Soda Computer"—named for their favorite beverage at the time. Wozniak later said of his first computer, "I wanted to design a machine that did something. On a TV, you turn a knob and it did something. On my computer, you pushed a few buttons and switches, and lights would come on."[4] It was not a very sophisticated machine, but Wozniak and Fernandez built it five years before the first kit for a home computer became available. Eventually

Fernandez invited Jobs to come see it. It was the first meeting between Jobs and Wozniak, but because of their differences in age and experience, they didn't click right away.

As Jobs progressed through high school, he became more and more interested in electronics and then computers. He also managed to get a summer job working at technology and computer company Hewlett-Packard's factory. Jobs had called one of the company's founders, Bill Hewlett, to ask for spare parts to use in a project, and Hewlett offered him the summer job.

Jobs graduated from high school in 1972. He decided to attend college at Reed

STEVE WOZNIAK

Stephen Gary Wozniak was born on August 11, 1950, in San Jose, California. His father, Jerry, worked for Lockheed Corporation, designing missile systems. The older Wozniak shared his interest in electronics with his son, who began tinkering with electronics at an early age. Once he reached high school, he excelled at electronics courses and later studied electrical engineering at the University of Colorado in Boulder. Wozniak dropped out of college in 1969 and began building his first computer from parts that had been rejected by various local companies because of their flaws. His "Cream Soda Computer" lasted only a short time before its power supply burned up, but it gave Wozniak a taste for computers. It was also at this time that he first met Jobs. Eventually the pair worked together to build a device that allowed phone calls to be made free of charge by copying signals used by the phone company. They quit building and selling the devices after encounters with the police and shady buyers. Jobs and Wozniak continued to cross paths for years. Some of their projects created bad feelings between them, but together they ultimately created Apple Computer.

College in Portland, Oregon. It was an extremely expensive school with a reputation for attracting brilliant and unique students. However, his first semester at Reed was a failure, and his grades were so poor that he dropped out of school and received a refund on his tuition. He also felt uncomfortable that his parents were spending so much money to send him to the school.

Instead of going home, Jobs hung around on campus, living in empty dorm rooms. He was also allowed to sit in on classes, the ones that really interested him, even though he could not take them for credit. Sitting in on a calligraphy class at Reed would later give him the idea of using multiple fonts in a computer, something no one had done before.

Jobs had discovered he could get an education on his own, at his own pace. But he was not sure what he wanted to do with his life. He read a great deal and meditated to determine what his path should be. In 1974, he decided to return home and move in with his parents. He would look for a job where he would make enough money to finance a trip to India. He hoped it would provide him with the answers he needed to move ahead in life. +

Jobs's summer working for Hewlett-Packard gave him valuable contacts and experience for the future.

Jobs and Wozniak were both involved in the early development of products for video game company Atari.

THE BIRTH OF APPLE

A fter returning to California, Jobs went looking for work. He found a job at the Atari video game company in 1974. Atari was founded in 1972 and was one of the first companies to manufacture video games. Jobs worked as a technician. Jobs's arrogant personality made it difficult for him to get along with the other employees, so much so that he worked nights only.

Meanwhile, in 1972, Wozniak had gotten a job with Hewlett-Packard's advanced product division making handheld calculators, which were a new technology at the time. Wozniak was still friends with Jobs, and Jobs was able to sneak him into the Atari headquarters after hours so Wozniak could play Atari's games for free. Wozniak was also available to help Jobs with technical problems beyond his expertise, such as designing a new video game. "Steve wasn't capable of designing anything that complex. He came to me and said Atari would like a game and described how it would work," Wozniak later recalled. "There was a catch: I had to do it in four days."[1] Wozniak was able to complete the new game, despite working full-time at Hewlett-Packard.

JOINING THE CLUB

A new computer club that would be integral to the creation of Apple started out with just a handwritten poster on notice boards at several local universities:

AMATEUR COMPUTER USERS GROUP AND HOMEBREW COMPUTER CLUB

Are you building your own computer?
Terminal? TV Typewriter? I/O Device?
Or some other digital black-magic box?
Or are you buying time on a time-sharing service?[2]

BONUS MONEY

When Jobs asked Wozniak to help him design the Atari game, *Breakout*, he told him they would split the bonus the company was offering, which Wozniak understood to be $700. He finished the game and eventually got his share of the money from Jobs. But years later, in 1984, Wozniak discovered from someone else that Jobs had actually received a $5,000 bonus for the game. Wozniak was not upset about the money because he had enjoyed the challenge of creating the game and said he would have done it for free. He was upset at being deceived by his friend, but he realized it was part of Jobs's business philosophy. According to Jobs, if you bought a part for thirty cents and sold it for six dollars, you didn't have to tell the buyer what it had cost you, because to him or her, it was worth six dollars. However, Wozniak did admit that if he had known about the incident earlier on, he might never have agreed to go into business with Jobs and form Apple Computer.

The first meeting of the Homebrew Computer Club took place on March 5, 1975, in a garage in Menlo Park, California. It was because of these meetings that Wozniak had an idea: he wanted to create a user-friendly desktop computer that would be available to people who were not computer hobbyists and did not want to build their own computer.

The MITS company in New Mexico had already created a new, smaller computer model that was different from the gigantic, noisy computers that filled an entire room. This new computer, the Altair (a name that came from the television series *Star Trek*), was the first truly desktop-sized computer, but it still looked daunting and difficult to use. Wozniak's idea was to design a computer that could use a standard typewriter QWERTY keyboard instead of switches to enter data, as the Altair did. And the computer would also be able to hook up to a regular television rather than an expensive printer or monitor.

MICROPROCESSOR CHIP

The invention that would change the course of computers from gigantic room-sized monsters to today's palm-sized tablets was the Intel microprocessor chip. The microprocessor is the brain of the computer that processes data. In 1971, Intel released its first chip, the Intel 4004. A few years later, it released the 8080 chip. These chips were smaller than previous chips, as well as more powerful and cheaper to manufacture. These tiny chips made personal computers possible, and they inspired Wozniak to build what became the Apple I computer.

THE APPLE I

On Sunday, June 29, 1975, after rounds of designing, programming, trying, and failing, Wozniak tried typing a few letters on his new computer, using the keyboard:

The Apple I was a basic circuit board
to which a user had to add a screen and keyboard.

I was shocked. The letters were displayed on the screen! . . . It was the first time in history anyone had typed a character on a keyboard and seen it show up on a screen right in front of them.[3]

The computer that would become the Apple I was born.

By March 1, 1976, Wozniak had completed the design for his new computer, and he showed it off at the next meeting of the Homebrew Computer Club. While Wozniak probably would have been happy to give away the schematic plans for it, Jobs immediately saw an opportunity for making money. He told Wozniak they should make and sell the printed circuit board that was the heart of the computer. "Steve didn't do one circuit design, or piece of code," Wozniak would later say. "But it never crossed my mind to sell computers. It was Steve who said 'Let's hold them up in the air and sell a few.'"[4]

Wozniak already had a good job at Hewlett-Packard, and he was not particularly interested in selling circuit boards instead. He did approach his employers, and Jobs approached Atari, to see if they would be interested in creating the microcomputers, the brand-new term for this generation of desktop computers. They showed off the prototype of Wozniak's computer, which was basically just a circuit board in a wooden case. Neither company was interested in producing the computer, so Jobs convinced Wozniak they should just go ahead and build the circuit

THE THIRD FOUNDER

Wozniak and Jobs knew they might need a third person who could mediate or cast a deciding vote if they disagreed with each other, so they brought in a third founder, Ronald Gerald Wayne. Wayne worked for Atari and had met Jobs there. However, Wayne withdrew from Apple Computer only two weeks after the company was formed, unwilling to take what he thought were considerable risks with the new company.

boards—not even complete computers—themselves. To make the money necessary to produce and sell the circuit boards, Jobs sold his Volkswagen Microbus for $1,500 and Wozniak sold his programmable HP calculator for $250.

They had a new company, but it needed a name. Wozniak remembers that Jobs thought up the name as they were driving along a highway in California one afternoon. Jobs had a group of friends who ran a farm in Oregon where he would work for a few months at a time. Wozniak said,

> We were driving along and he said "I've got a great name: Apple Computer."... Both of us tried to think of a technical-sounding mixture of words, like Executek and Matrix Electronics, but after ten minutes of trying, we both realized that we weren't going to beat Apple Computer.[5]

The official founding day of Apple Computer was April 1, 1976. Now that they had a company, Jobs went looking for customers. He and Wozniak planned to sell the bare circuit boards for $50 each, assuming the hobbyists who purchased them would fill in the rest of the necessary equipment to create an actual computer. With the first batch of printed circuit boards ready, he demonstrated one of the

Apple I computers at a Homebrew Club meeting. The computer caught the eye of Paul Jay Terrell, who ran a chain of computer stores called the Byte Shop. Jobs convinced Terrell to place an order, but there was a catch: Terrell didn't just want plain circuit boards. He wanted 50 fully assembled computers. Wozniak would later say, "That was the biggest single episode in all of the company's history. Nothing in subsequent years was so great and so unexpected. It was not what we had expected to do."[6]

Apple Computer did not have enough money to build the 50 computers, but that did not stop Jobs. He got a loan for $5,000 to buy parts. They couldn't afford to rent a space for assembly, so they used Jobs's parents' garage in Los Altos. They also stored and assembled some parts in spare bedrooms. Jobs's sister Patty did some of the assembly work. Wozniak said, "We were real small-time operators, kind of like somebody who sold arts and crafts on the side."[7] They also hired their old friend Bill Fernandez as their first real full-time employee.

COLLECTIBLE COMPUTER

Original Apple I computers have been highly collectible souvenirs. In 1999, an Apple I—complete with the user manual, keyboard, a homemade case, and the original $600 check that paid for the computer—was sold at auction for $18,000. In 2002, another working Apple I sold for $14,000.

However, the first delivery of product to the Byte Shop was not complete computers as expected, but only the circuit boards. The shop was forced to finish the computers by putting them in handmade cases, as well as supplying power supplies and keyboards. Regardless of the fact that they had not exactly delivered what had been ordered, Jobs and Wozniak made approximately $8,000 in profit. Apple Computer was on its way. +

At a 2010 conference, Jobs revisits the past,
presenting a 30-year-old image of himself and Wozniak.

The Apple II was more user-friendly than the Apple I.

FROM THE GARAGE TO THE WORLD

Jobs and Wozniak had launched their new company and fulfilled—at least in part—their first order. But the Apple I computer was not a complete success. Computer hobbyists were disappointed the new computer did not run on the new Intel 8080 microprocessor chip. It was also not ready to use at the time of purchase because it still needed an interface that would add the BASIC computer language to run the computer. And before BASIC could even be loaded, the computer had to be painstakingly programmed with data entered by hand. Finally, Wozniak solved that problem by creating a $75 card that plugged into the computer's expansion slot (much like a USB port on today's computers) and allowed users to load programs stored on standard cassette audiotapes.

THE APPLE II

Wozniak kept working on his computer, and soon he had a prototype of what would eventually be the Apple II computer. However, it was clear the improved computer would cost several hundred dollars each to produce, much more than the Apple I computer. And Apple did not have the money to make them. It needed financial help.

Wozniak and Jobs were then lucky enough to meet Mike Markkula, a marketing specialist and venture capitalist, someone who lends money to help new businesses get started. He agreed to lend them $250,000 to incorporate their company and

Jobs and Wozniak debuted the Apple II
at the West Coast Computer Faire in 1977.

perfect the improved Apple II. In return, Markkula
would get a one-third ownership in the company.
However, one of his conditions was that Wozniak
would stop working for Hewlett-Packard, since that
company could claim the rights to his computer
inventions while he was still employed by them.
Although Wozniak liked his job there, he agreed and
quit to work full-time for Apple. The final piece of
the puzzle was to hire someone to act as president
of Apple, since none of the others had experience in
actually running a company. Markkula brought on

Michael Scott, who was previously the director of manufacturing at National Semiconductor.

On April 17, 1977, at the first West Coast Computer Faire in San Francisco, the Apple II computer was introduced to the public. Apple II was a huge success because it was aimed at a mass market. It came with a case, a standard keyboard, and a power supply, and it was capable of displaying color graphics. And even at a price of $1,298, three times the cost of an Apple I, the computer was hugely successful.

Soon, the Disk II became available and made the Apple II an even greater success. It was a floppy disk drive—a form of data storage that came before compact discs (CDs)—that plugged into one of the Apple II's expansion slots and gave it better storage capacity than any other computer, especially since computers still stored data on audiotape cassettes. Software engineers were also working on spreadsheet "calculator" applications for computers, and when Apple introduced the Apple II Plus

MACS IN SCHOOLS

By the end of the 1970s, high schools around the country started teaching students how to use BASIC programming as part of their curriculum, feeling students would need this skill in the future. This helped create a huge educational market for the Apple II. In addition, once students used the computers at school, they began asking for them from their parents as gifts. This unexpected market helped keep Apple going during the early years of the Apple II.

The Apple II could read original floppy discs, *left*. The first Macintosh, introduced in 1984, used smaller discs, *right*. CDs, *bottom*, became popular in the late 1990s.

computer in June 1979, it came with the Disk II and also included VisiCalc, an electronic spreadsheet. It would make it possible for the computer to become a business tool as well as a home tool. Because VisiCalc ran only on Apple computers, sales of Apple II took off.

CHANGING IMAGES

Wozniak continued to be the brains behind Apple
Computer. Jobs was the public face, the one who
went out and got funding and created the company's
advertising. As a result of the company's growing
stature, Jobs needed to give himself a makeover. He
was used to looking rather scruffy with long hair,
jeans, and a T-shirt. He had once shown up for a
meeting with a potential investor in his bare feet.
Now he deliberately changed his appearance in order
to appeal to young professional businessmen, whom
he considered to be
Apple's potential users.
He kept his long hair,
but trimmed it, and he
now wore a suit. Yet he
still had a reputation
for not always being
very pleasant for his
employees to work with.

Wozniak,
meanwhile, continued
to tweak and improve
the basic design of the
Apple II, although some

CREATING A LOGO

In 1977, Jobs hired Regis McKenna Inc. to
design a new logo for Apple Computer. Art director Rob Janoff started with a black-and-white
silhouette of an apple, but it needed more. "I
wanted to simplify the shape of an apple," he
said, "and by taking a bite—a byte, right?—out
of the side, it prevented the apple from looking
like a cherry tomato."[1] Jobs insisted Janoff add
six horizontal colorful stripes inside the apple, in
tribute to the color graphic capacity of the computer. These stripes, which did not have black
lines separating them, made reproducing the
logo more complicated and more expensive. The
logo was further simplified in 1999, when it was
changed to solid white.

people in the company wondered if their success was going to be short-lived without new products. The company was working on the Apple III, which would be intended for the business market while the Apple II remained a product for homes and schools.

Meanwhile, the company itself was growing and changing. In the summer of 1978, a little more than a year after the introduction of the Apple II, the company was building approximately 30 computers a day. There were 28 people and a supervisor in the manufacturing department, but Apple needed more employees every day. They often lured away employees from other companies such as Intel or Hewlett-Packard. They were also being forced to operate like a big company rather than a group of people making computers in a garage. They needed people to oversee quality control and design and to engineer hardware. Projects and schedules needed to be formalized and controlled, and forms and meetings became a way of life. One young engineer at Apple resented the changes, saying, "We thought 'Here we go. Here comes the red tape and forms to fill out and meetings every week.' Organization was just too hard to take."[2]

The company was growing quickly. In just three years, by September 1980, 130,000 Apple II computers had been sold. Annual revenue was now $11.7 million. Apple's payroll now boasted 1,000 employees, and the company occupied 15 buildings in Silicon Valley, most of them in Cupertino.

GOING PUBLIC

On December 12, 1980, Apple Computer took another step and went public, meaning shares in the company would now be traded on the New York Stock Exchange and investors could buy those shares and essentially own a small part of the company. The price of a single share of Apple stock was priced at $22, and all 4.6 million shares sold out in just minutes. The net worth of the company quickly grew to approximately $1.78 billion. Overnight, many of the Apple founders and employees became millionaires. Jobs's own net worth was more than $100 million after the 1980 sale of stock.

OVERNIGHT MILLIONAIRES

When Apple went public in 1980, more than 100 people became millionaires overnight. Many of these employees had never before made salaries of more than $40,000 in a year.

THE WOZ PLAN

Wozniak always felt it was unfair that some of Apple's employees were not given stock options, the opportunity to buy company stock. He felt he had more money than he could use, so when the company was about to go public, he sold one-third of his stock to Apple employees at low prices through something he called the Woz Plan.

It had been a fast and furious ride from a garage in Los Altos to a company worth billions of dollars. But as with any ride, there were bound to be bumps along the way, and soon Apple would encounter some of them. +

The Apple II was key to Jobs's and Apple Computer's early success.

Jobs and an Apple technician show off
their newest computer model, Lisa, in 1983.

GROWING PAINS

F or years, Apple was the standout company in
personal computers. But the company leaders
were smart enough to realize that sooner
or later they would have competition, and they
were fairly certain they knew where it would come

from. On August 12, 1981, International Business
Machines (IBM) released its own personal computer.
Priced at $1,565, it had a single 5.25-inch (13-cm)
floppy drive and 16K of memory.

At first, Apple was very accommodating. It even
took out a full-page ad in the *Wall Street Journal*,
welcoming IBM to the market for personal computers.
However, it also considered the IBM computer to
be inferior to the Apple II. Jobs said, "It's curious
to me that the largest computer company in the
world couldn't even match the Apple II, which was
designed in a garage six years ago."[1] But even if the
first IBM computer could not outdo the Apple II, it
did have the power of a known and trusted company
name. By the end of its first year,
IBM had sold 50,000 computers,
and Apple's share of the computer
market was flat while IBM's grew.

THE LISA

In January 1983, Apple tried to
regain some of its importance in the
computer market by introducing
a new computer, the Lisa. Jobs
had been interested in creating a

A DANGEROUS ACCIDENT

In early 1981, Wozniak was
nearly killed when the private
plane he was piloting crashed.
He suffered severe facial
injuries, a concussion, and a
period of amnesia. He took a
leave of absence from Apple in
March 1981 and didn't return
for one year.

computer that was even more user-friendly than the Apple II, which still required users to enter commands using a keyboard. The Lisa would use a new device to control the computer, inspired by one Jobs had seen on a visit to the Xerox Corporation: a new pointing device, the three-button mouse, which had been invented in the 1960s. When the Lisa was introduced it was equipped with a redesigned one-button mouse. The Lisa also came with seven software applications, including spreadsheets, a word processor, and a drawing program. Unfortunately, it also had a price to match: $9,995. This put the new computer out of reach of the

COMPANY VALUES

In the 1980s, Apple made a list of its company values:

- "One person, one computer

- We are going for it, and we will set aggressive goals

- We build products we believe in

- We are here to make a positive difference in society, as well as make a profit

- Each person is important; each has the opportunity and the obligation to make a difference

- We are all in it together, win or lose

- We are enthusiastic!

- We are creative: we set the pace

- We want everyone to enjoy the adventure we are on together

- We care about what we do

- We want to create an environment in which Apple values flourish"[2]

average consumer and made it affordable only to businesses. The Lisa had also cost millions of dollars in development and came in over budget and behind schedule. On top of everything, its processor was slow, and the floppy disk drive system was unreliable. However, its biggest problem in the marketplace was one Apple could blame only itself for: the launch of the Macintosh on January 24, 1984.

THE MACINTOSH

As early as 1979, Apple chairman Mike Markkula had asked employee Jef Raskin if he wanted to work on a new Apple project, code-named "Annie," which was to create a $400 computer specifically for gaming. Apple already had its expensive Apple II and the extremely expensive Lisa in development, so the company needed another option on the market. This new computer would be for the average person. It would be completely contained in a case with no extra cables so it would be more easily portable. Ultimately, the Macintosh, or Mac, would have many of the same features as the Lisa, but at a much more affordable price. Part of the reason for this was that Jobs, who had been edged out of the Lisa project after it failed to generate expected sales, insisted on

CRITICAL APPEAL

Many critics weighed in at the launch of the Macintosh, including Bob Ryan of *inCider* magazine in March 1984:"[The Macintosh] is a machine which will appeal to the masses of people who have neither the time nor the inclination to embark upon the long learning process required to master the intricacies of the present generation of personal computers. . . . The Macintosh should establish itself as the next standard in personal computers."[4]

helping with the development of the Macintosh. He introduced an element of competition between the Lisa and the Macintosh, boasting that the Mac would be as good as the Lisa but at a much lower price. He ended up creating a rift in Apple between those who were working on the Lisa and the Macintosh, and those who worked on the Apple II felt ignored.

Raskin also had trouble working with Jobs. He said, "[Jobs] would try to push himself into everything. No matter what you were doing, he had to have something to do with it. Nobody at Apple wanted him involved with their projects. I had started the Macintosh team and we didn't want him either."[3] But when the Macintosh finally debuted, Jobs delivered the announcement and excited the crowd about the new product. At the Apple shareholder meeting on January 24, 1984, he announced:

"There have only been two milestone products so far in our industry. The Apple II in 1977, and the IBM PC in 1981. Today . . . we are introducing the third industry milestone, Macintosh."[5] Jobs then pulled the Macintosh computer out of a canvas bag sitting on a table, and demonstrated its graphics and voice synthesizer. However, the price was significantly higher than the $400 Apple had originally intended. The Macintosh debuted at $2,495.

"1984"

The Macintosh was announced through a television commercial shown during Super Bowl XVIII on January 22, 1984. This commercial, which was loosely modeled on the book *1984* by George Orwell, shows an athletic woman with a sledgehammer being chased by uniformed men. She enters an

MACINTOSH SPEAKS

At the launch of the new Macintosh computer, the computer itself "spoke" to the audience to demonstrate its synthesized voice: "Hello. I am Macintosh. It sure is great to get out of that bag. Unaccustomed as I am to public speaking, I'd like to share with you a thought that occurred to me that first time I met an IBM mainframe: Never trust a computer you can't lift. But right now I'd like to sit back and listen. So it is with considerable pride that I introduce a man who has been like a father to me, Steve Jobs."[6]

1984

The novel *1984* was written by British author George Orwell in 1949. It tells the story of a dystopian society where mind control and government surveillance control citizens and subdue them for the greater good. A political leader known as Big Brother heads the country. In Apple's "1984" commercial, the face on the screen is similar to Big Brother. The underlying message is that individual consumers should break away from what Big Brother, or IBM, is telling them to do and use the new Macintosh computer instead.

auditorium where rows and rows of drone-like workers are watching a huge face talking on a screen. The woman, wearing a Mac T-shirt, hits the screen with her sledgehammer, and a burst of light surrounds the workers. During the closing shot, a voice says, "On January 24th, Apple Computer will introduce Macintosh. And you'll see why 1984 won't be like '1984.'"[7]

However, it seemed the new Macintosh would not be enough to keep Apple healthy. The new computer was not selling in the huge numbers Apple had anticipated. Apple's percentage of the market had shrunk as the IBM PC and similar computers had taken more of the market share. Apple reported a huge financial loss for the fourth quarter of 1983, so the value of its stocks plummeted. Because of this loss, Jobs saw his personal net worth drop $250 million in just a few weeks.

The Macintosh was not popular enough
to repair Apple's declining success.

CHANGES

In April 1983, Jobs recruited John Sculley, former
CEO of soft-drink company PepsiCo Inc, to become
Apple's new CEO. He knew the company needed a
fresh perspective from someone who had not been
involved in the computer industry before. Sculley
came in at a time when Apple was starting to go
downhill financially, and he also began having
difficulties dealing with Jobs. Sculley finally asked
Apple's executives to choose sides—with him or
with Jobs—and more conflict grew between the two

men and their supporters within the company. Jobs tried to get the other executives to vote Sculley out of the company, but they would not. Jobs was left without any real role in his own company. Finally, on September 17, 1985, Jobs officially resigned from Apple. He said:

> *I feel like somebody just punched me in the stomach and knocked all my wind out. I'm only 30 years old and I want to have a chance to continue creating things. I know I've got at least one more great computer in me. And Apple is not going to give me a chance to do that.*[8]

Apple and Jobs would now be going their separate ways . . . at least for a while. +

John Sculley, shown with the Macintosh II in 1987,
led Apple after Jobs left the company.

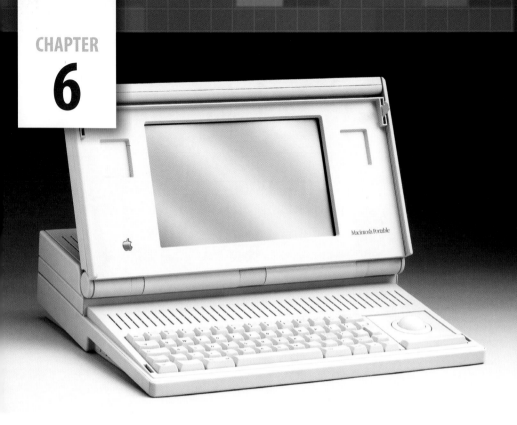

The Macintosh Portable was Apple's forerunner to a laptop computer.

APPLE'S NeXT STEP

J obs was out of the equation, and Apple entered a period of struggle. Many people began to wonder if the company was just one more tech business destined to come and go and then be forgotten. Jobs himself started a new company in

January 1986, called NeXT, and he was involved in creating a computer that could be used in universities and for scientific applications.

GOING PORTABLE

But Apple was not completely dead. It was still creating new products, and one of those was the idea of a "Mac in a book," which was supposed to be the next logical step in making a Mac computer easily portable. In September 1989, the new product was introduced to the world: the Macintosh Portable, with a price tag of $6,500. It had innovative features such as a full-sized keyboard and a trackball instead of a mouse. But it also had a major problem. It weighed approximately 16 pounds (7 kg), almost as much as the original Macintosh desktop. This was a time when competing companies were making laptops that weighed closer to ten pounds (5 kg), although the Macintosh Portable was more powerful than its lightweight competition.

In 1991, Apple released the PowerBook. Designed to be just as powerful as a desktop Mac, it was more portable than the bulky Macintosh Portable. It was also more successful.

APPLE'S NEWTON

Apple CEO Sculley had another new project he hoped would bring revenue to Apple, which was continuing to suffer from declining sales and increased competition. He wanted Apple to become part of the new personal digital assistant (PDA) market, creating a small, portable computer message pad operated with a pen-like stylus. The Newton would allow its users to keep track of appointments on a calendar, write notes and to-do lists, and perform other basic applications similar to what today's BlackBerry and iPhone can do. It

THE NeXT CUBE

In the fall of 1989, Jobs released the NeXT Cube computer. It had some different innovations, not the least of which was its unusual cube shape. The most important innovation was the NeXT Cube's new kind of programming, object-oriented programming (OOP). This kind of programming meant that different programs could share information and features, and programmers could create relationships between the different pieces, or objects, of the system. It was also a more flexible type of programming, since it allowed programmers to make changes to one part of the operating system without changing everything, because each function of the computer is its own module. In an interview with *Rolling Stone* magazine in 1994, Jobs said, "In my 20 years in this industry, I have never seen a revolution as profound as this. You can build software literally five to 10 times faster, and that software is much more reliable, much easier to maintain and much more powerful."[1] However, the cube design for the NeXT Cube made it difficult to fit all the parts into the computer. It was also more than $6,000, more than most individuals or schools could afford.

was also supposed to translate handwritten notes into typed text, but the software for this application did not work well. Apple teamed with other electronics companies, including Motorola and Sharp, to help construct the devices.

The Newton was released in 1993. It had some initial bugs, but it received several technology awards. It quickly pushed other companies to develop their own versions of a PDA. The technology involved in the Newton products would also lead the company toward the eventual creation of the iPhone and the iPad.

The Newton's eventual success brought some much-needed money to Apple, but by 1997, Apple spun off the Newton division as its own company. The continuing decline of Apple's share of the computer marketplace had forced Sculley to resign in 1993, and the head of Apple Europe, Michael Spindler, had replaced him without improving the company's economic situation. The new Apple CEO Gilbert Amelio, who joined the company in 1996, said, "Keeping Newton alive had been costing Apple some $15 million a quarter . . . but . . . with the MessagePad 2000, Newton was breaking even and poised to be a money-earner for the company."[2] The Newton became a subsidiary of Apple, one that

The Newton enjoyed some success
but ultimately was unprofitable for Apple.

Apple owned completely but operated as a separate business.

By February 1998, however, Apple announced it would no longer be developing any further Newton devices. Despite the popularity of the handheld computers, ultimately the Newton was not worth the $500 million Apple had spent on development and marketing. As the lead engineer on the Newton project, Steve Capps, said, "Whether or not the product succeeded, we helped set up a category. . . . You have to be bold to make bold jumps. When you succeed, you're everybody's favorite hero, and when you fail, you're everybody's [scape]goat."[3]

OTHER FALSE STARTS

Throughout the 1990s, Apple tried other new products to regain some of its strength in the marketplace. Efforts included the Centris and Quadra lines of computers. Another attempt was the Performa line, a series of consumer-oriented computers sold through stores such as Sears and Walmart. Most of the Performa computers were simply other Apple models that had been repackaged or slightly tweaked. In order to minimize competition between the stores, Apple packaged the Performa computers with different bundles of software and features so that each store had a specific model to sell. Unfortunately, consumers were often confused by the differences, and salespeople in the stores were not properly trained to answer their questions. It was also difficult to get service for the computers, since the stores where they were sold were not authorized service centers.

Apple also experimented with other consumer electronics, such as television accessories, video game consoles, and digital cameras.

"Apple has been a somewhat dysfunctional world, arrogant when it was most successful and wonderfully innovative when its back was up against the wall."[4]

—*John Sculley,*
former Apple CEO

Between 1994 and 1996, Apple also operated an Internet portal called eWorld. It included an e-mail service, a news service, and online bulletin boards. It was expensive compared to other Internet services, and it never attracted very many users.

Apple was under increasing competition from IBM and its PC and Microsoft Windows–based computers. By 1996, the Mac operating system needed improvement, particularly to regain some of the market share that had been lost to Windows-running computers. Rather than going to the expense of building its own new system at a time when the company was in rocky shape, Apple once again looked to the work of the man who had helped create the company. Jobs had developed a powerful operating system for his own line of computers, NeXTSTEP. Would it also be the next step to save Apple? +

Jobs unveiled his NeXT computer in October 1988.

Apple CEO Amelio oversaw the purchase of NeXT
but was soon replaced by Jobs.

BACK TO APPLE

Jobs had spent the years after his resignation from Apple working on his new computer project, NeXT. He had secured new funding from investors such as billionaire H. Ross Perot and Stanford University. He even paid a huge sum of money to have a new logo designed for his company. However, NeXT was never a successful business, and by 1996 it was in decline, just when Apple needed a new operating system for its computers.

MAKING A DEAL

Jobs went to work. He heard Apple was analyzing four other companies' software, including Microsoft. He decided to convince Apple it should purchase NeXT and utilize its software. He argued that his software was superior to everything else, and that if Apple purchased his company, it would immediately have the benefit of NeXT's 300 employees.

Apple's CEO Amelio agreed, and in 1996 Apple bought NeXT for $337.5 million in cash and 1.5 million shares of stock for Jobs. NeXT was now part of Apple, and Jobs was back as a special adviser. However, as the company continued its record of dismal performance, Jobs replaced Amelio in July 1997. Jobs served as interim CEO until September 16, when he became permanent CEO.

JOBS'S FAMILY

Jobs always kept his personal life extremely private. He married Laurene Powell in 1991. They had three children, Reed Powell, Erin Sienna, and Eve, whom they kept out of the spotlight. In addition, Jobs had a daughter, Lisa Brennan-Jobs, with his high school girlfriend in 1978.

Jobs was back at the head of Apple, but he would have to work hard to keep Apple afloat. As author Michael Moritz wrote in his book *Return to the Little Kingdom*:

> *The Apple [Jobs] inherited in the fall of 1997 had lost its creative zest and leadership position in the technology industry, was almost out of cash, was unable to [acquire] young engineers, was drowning in inventory of unsold computers, and had nothing imaginative in the works.*[1]

The computer market was at the time dominated by PCs running Microsoft MS-DOS operating systems. Apple still controlled a good share of the educational market, but only one in 20 individual computer users was using a Mac. The company had lost $1 billion in 1996 alone.

Jobs immediately put into place measures that did not make him popular but were meant to save the company. He cut costs, laid off a substantial number of employees, and killed product lines he did not believe were working or contributing to the company, such as the Newton PDA line and a line of printers. He also stopped allowing other manufacturers to use the Macintosh operating system and limited how many vendors could sell Apple products.

THE APPLE STORE

Another innovation for the new era of Apple was the 2001 opening of the first Apple store. It was conceived as a way to give Apple back more of the computer market share and to fight against the poor marketing Apple was getting from the retail stores, which were its authorized distributors. Apple's 2005 company report gave some of the reasons behind creating the retail stores:

One of the goals of the retail initiative is to bring new customers to the Company and expand its installed base through sales to computer users who currently do not own a Macintosh computer and first time personal computer buyers. By operating its own stores and building them

BETTER MARKETING

One of the marketing initiatives Jobs used to bring Apple back into the front of the computer industry was the "Think Different" campaign, which debuted in 1997. It used a series of black-and-white portraits of famous inventive and artistic people, such as musicians John Lennon, Bob Dylan, and Louis Armstrong; architect Frank Lloyd Wright; scientists Albert Einstein and Thomas Edison; moviemaker Jim Henson; and adventurer Amelia Earhart. According to Michael Moritz in *Return to the Little Kingdom*, "The campaign was a rallying cry, but it was also a keen expression of the artistic, sensuous, romantic, mystical, inquisitive, and theatrical side of Jobs—adjectives not usually associated with the leader of a technology company. It was these attributes that eventually came to be expressed in Apple's products."[2] Even today, Apple has a reputation as the computer of choice for creative people such as writers, filmmakers, and designers.

Apple is known for its clean and uncluttered stores.

in desirable high traffic locations, the Company is able to better control the customer retail experience and attract new customers. The stores are designed to simplify and enhance the presentation and marketing of personal computing products. The stores provide a forum in which the Company is able to present computing solutions to users in areas such as digital photography, digital video, music, children's software, and home and small business computing.[3]

The stores would be a challenge at first. Ron Johnson, who was hired as vice president of retail at Apple in 2000, remembered talking with Jobs about the new retail store idea. Johnson quickly realized the 6,000 square feet (557 sq m) of each store would be a challenge to fill, considering Apple had only four products to sell—two portable devices and two desktop computers. He explained,

> *That was a challenge. But it ended up being the ultimate opportunity, because we said, because we don't have enough products to fill a store that size, let's fill it with the ownership experience.*[4]

The first two Apple stores opened in Virginia and California in 2001. The Apple stores were very successful, and by 2007 their sales per square foot of store were greater than that of stores such as Best Buy and Tiffany & Co. Five years later Apple opened its flagship store in New York City. The store's entrance is through a huge glass cube with the Apple logo located on the plaza outside the store.

THE iMAC

On August 15, 1998, Apple released a new computer, the iMac. The iMac had an egg-shaped plastic case that came in several different colors, instead of the square, beige cases most computers came in. It was the first Macintosh computer to have a Universal Serial Bus (USB) port that made it easy to plug in

A SUPER WEAPON

Apple debuted the Power Mac G4 computer in 1999. It was the first personal computer powerful enough to be classified as a "supercomputer," and thus identified as a weapon by the US government. This restricted the computer from being sold in certain countries. Apple utilized this designation in a commercial that showed a G4 computer surrounded by tanks.

devices such as printers. Many personal computers already had USB ports and could now easily adapt their accessories to fit Macs as well. The iMac came with everything the user needed to go online, all contained inside the case. Even the monitor was combined with the other computer elements, rather than using a separate tower. The average consumer could open the box, plug in the computer, and start using the Internet right away.

The iMac was the phenomenal success Apple needed. Due partly to a great marketing campaign, it had 150,000 preorders and became the fastest-selling personal computer in history. More than 2 million iMacs were sold in just one year. The iMac was followed by the portable iBook in 1999, which came with an option called AirPort for wireless networking and was also widely successful.

Apple was back to being a leader in the computer industry. But there were other, even greater innovations in its future. +

The iMac was brightly colored and user-friendly.

The original iPod had raised buttons.

THE AGE OF iTUNES

I n 2000, most people listened to music recorded on CDs, but some still used cassette tapes and even vinyl records. Common portable forms of music were Walkman portable cassette players, Discman CD players, and small portable radios. An encoding format called MP3 was used to store music and other audio digitally, but the few MP3 players that did exist were cumbersome and difficult to use. At this same time, Jobs was searching for new products that could expand Apple's range in the marketplace.

The iPOD

The answer was the iPod. Jobs was never very interested in the Apple Newton PDA, but he wondered if perhaps a similar kind of personal computing device could be used for music. People who loved listening to music had already figured out they could put music from CDs onto their computers and transform them into MP3 digital files that could then be played from the computer, sort of like a new kind of stereo system. It required a software program to make the conversion from CD to MP3 file, but several companies had created this software. The best program was called SoundJam MP, created

"Not so long ago we listened to music on the go with a cassette-based Walkman and, later, a portable CD player. Inevitably you'd have to untangle the magnetically coated tape from the grasps of your heavy Walkman or restart your CD after going over a major bump in the road while riding in the backseat of your parents' car. As we celebrate the 10 year anniversary of the Apple iPod, it's hard to believe what we were putting up with before it arrived."[1]

—PC Magazine *author*
Jennifer Bergen

by a company called Casady & Greene (C&G). Some of Apple's industry scouts had seen SoundJam MP. Apple already had some ties with C&G through computer games the company had created for Apple. Apple's engineering staff had helped C&G create and develop a new program for better digital music software, and eventually Apple offered to buy the rights to SoundJam.

At the same time Apple was acquiring SoundJam, college student Shawn Fanning was working out a new way to download free music from the Internet. Fanning perfected the art of using MP3 technology to compress digital music files so they could be downloaded more quickly and easily. Eventually Fanning started a

MP3 FILES

What exactly does MP3 mean, and what is an MP3 file? MP3 was developed by the Moving Picture Experts Group (MPEG), a group of European engineers who created a set of standards for translating picture and sound into digital files. Engineers developed the MP3 (short for MPEG Audio Layer 3) as a way to make digital files smaller while still maintaining good sound quality. They eliminated the very high and very low sounds from a digital sound file, sounds which a listener would not have heard anyway because they lie outside the range of normal human hearing. These digital files could then be compressed into smaller files. They could be circulated on the Internet and played on any computer. Unlike previous innovations in music technology, such as vinyl record albums and cassette tapes, MP3 technology became popular thanks to the efforts of people who listened to music via the Internet, rather than the efforts of the music industry itself.

Web site where music files could be stored and swapped, and soon millions of songs were available for free. The site would be called Napster. However, Napster faced major legal repercussions since these music downloads were essentially stealing music consumers would otherwise have had to buy from music companies and artists. Apple and its iPod would soon provide consumers with a legal alternative to Web sites such as Napster.

In January 2001, Jobs attended the Macworld Expo to introduce a new product. It would successfully combine the MP3 technology of tiny compressed digital music files with the ability to create a personal library of songs. And it would be a free download for Mac users. Its name was iTunes. Jobs told his audience, "Apple has done what Apple does best—make complex applications easy, and make them even more powerful in the process. iTunes is miles ahead of every other jukebox application, and we hope its

KEEPING THE iPOD A SECRET

Jobs was determined to keep details about Apple's new iPod undercover until the product was released. As a result, during the testing phase, the prototype iPod was often concealed in a box the size of a shoebox. Wires for the controls would be placed at random spots on the box's exterior: the screen might be on top, and the scroll wheel might be on the side. By hiding the actual iPod this way, no competitor would be able to tell exactly how the finished product would look until it was officially unveiled.

dramatically simpler user interface will bring even more people into the digital music revolution."[2]

Once Apple had its iTunes software in place, it was natural for the company to think about creating a better machine for utilizing the MP3 files than what was already on the market. Apple employee Tony Fadell already had the idea for an MP3 player design. Gradually, with input from Jobs, Fadell created the first iPod. It was approximately the size of a person's palm, with a display window, a scroll wheel instead of push buttons for controls, and enough memory for thousands of songs. One of Jobs's specifications for the device was that it shouldn't require more than three pushes of a control button to get to a particular song.

At its introduction on October 23, 2001, Jobs said, "Apple has invented a whole new category of digital music players that lets you put your entire music collection in your pocket and listen to it wherever you go."[3] With an iPod, a user could easily download music from the iTunes application on a Mac computer with very little user effort, though the device was not compatible with other computers until its second generation redesign. Jobs finished by saying, "With iPod, listening to music will never be the same again."[4]

At first, the iPod was not wildly successful, especially with its price of $399, but by 2002, more than 200,000 iPods were purchased during the fourth quarter of that year alone. Soon the iPod was outselling Apple's computers, and it was expected that it and the iTunes Store would soon account for half of the company's revenue. Apple would continue to bring out newer iPods with different memory capacities, sizes, shapes, and colors.

THE iTUNES STORE

The third part of the iPod success was the creation of an Apple iTunes Music Store, where songs could be purchased as MP3s. It was a similar idea to Fanning's Napster site, but it would require the user to actually buy the music instead of downloading it for free, as was possible on Napster. Illegal music swapping on sites such as Napster

"Music is so deep within all of us, but it's easy to go for a day or week or month or year without really listening to music. The iPod has changed that for millions of people, and that makes me really happy because I think music is good for the soul."[5]

—*Steve Jobs*

iTunes was immediately popular with Apple customers.

was hurting the music industry, and those types of sites would eventually be shut down.

In order to use iTunes technology for legal music downloading, Jobs had to go to five of the major music companies—Sony, Warner, EMI, Universal, and BMG—and get them to agree to allow iTunes to distribute their music over the Internet. Since these five companies controlled most of the popular music in the world, much of the music iPod users wanted would become available to download legally for a small fee, usually 99¢ for a song and

$9.99 for an entire album. The music companies, in turn, would receive a fee from Apple.

The five companies eventually agreed, but only after Apple agreed to use technologies that would prevent songs from being shared illegally. For example, if a user tried to download someone else's songs from that person's computer to the user's own iPod, a message would appear, saying if the new songs were loaded, all the previous music would be erased from the iPod. It was a simple way to prevent illegal sharing.

The iTunes Store debuted on April 28, 2003, and its popularity proved that music lovers would quickly adopt this new system of music distribution.

A NAME CHANGE

By 2006, Apple was making more money from its music products than from its computers. During one

JOBS'S HEALTH DECLINES

In 2004, Jobs was diagnosed with pancreatic cancer. Jobs refused to follow conventional medical treatments such as surgery and instead focused on more natural treatments for cancer such as special diets, herbal remedies, and acupuncture. He did ultimately have surgery, but not until nine months after his diagnosis. It was a decision he supposedly later regretted as the cancer became more invasive.

three-month period, Apple sold more than $3 billion worth of iPods, music, and accessories, while during the same time it sold only $2 billion worth of computers. As a result of this shift, in early 2007, Jobs decided it was time for a name change. From then on, Apple Computer would be known as Apple Inc. This change reflected not only the current shift in products but also the direction the company would continue to take in the future. +

Jobs announced further improvements to the iPod in 2004,
including the iPod mini.

Since its introduction in 2007,
the iPhone has become indispensable for many.

IN THE PALM OF YOUR HAND

N ow Apple Inc., the tremendous success of the iPod proved the company had found a niche that went beyond laptop computers. This would become even more evident with Apple's next new product: the iPhone.

STARTING WITH A NOTION

Like many of Apple and Jobs's ideas, the iPhone started with an observation: in 2007, computer companies were spending a lot of money developing smaller and lighter computers called tablet PCs, which were very thin and portable and controlled with a touch screen rather than a mouse and keyboard. At the same time, the market for cell phones was growing at a tremendous rate. Jobs had already asked his engineers to come up with a better touch screen for small tablet computers, and then he had the notion that perhaps the best new technology might combine a tablet touch screen computer with a cell phone. The result was the iPhone.

As often happened in the past, the iPhone started with Jobs's idea that if something did not work well, then he should try to fix it. According to Lev Grossman in *Time* magazine:

> *[In 2007] cell phones interested Jobs because even though they do all kinds of stuff—calling, text messaging, Web browsing, contact management,*

"The iPhone—and later the iPad—were glorious expressions of Apple's approach to product design. [They] began with a few people trying to design a product they would want to use and be proud to own."[1]

—*Michael Moritz,*
Return to the Little Kingdom

music playback, how-tos and video—they do it very badly, by forcing you to press lots of tiny buttons . . . and squint at a tiny screen. "Everybody hates their phone," Jobs says, "and that's not a good thing. And there's an opportunity there." To Jobs' perfectionist eyes, phones are broken. Jobs likes things that are broken. It means he can make something that isn't and sell it to you at a premium price.[2]

Basically, the iPhone combined features from the iPod with a real computer operating system that enabled the user to surf the Internet and use e-mail and various other applications for gaming, social networking, and GPS, all with a touch screen and a bright, easy-to-read display. Jobs, as always, was the one to announce the new iPhone at the 2007 Macworld convention on January 9, saying, "Today Apple is going to reinvent the phone."[3]

The iPhone was an immediate success, despite a $499 price tag, and potential customers lined up outside Apple stores to purchase them. Apple had announced special store hours and also limited the purchase of iPhones to a strict two per customer. Owning an iPhone became the new status symbol for early adopters, people who liked to be the first in

Customers waited outside Apple stores
for days in order to purchase the iPhone.

their circle of friends to own new technology. Even the problems with iPhone service early on did not deter its fans.

COMPUTERS TO GO

But in typical Apple and Jobs fashion, the next big thing was already in the works. The iPhone developed out of a market for small, portable tablet computers that could be used almost anywhere. But Jobs and his company knew sometimes there was a need for a device that was larger than the iPhone, particularly for reading magazines or books and for playing games, multimedia, and music. On

January 27, 2010—the 130th anniversary of the day Thomas Edison filed his patent for the electric incandescent lightbulb—Jobs announced the iPad during a press conference in San Francisco. Jobs later said of the iPad, "When people see how immersive the experience is, how directly you engage with it . . . the only word is magical."[4]

The iPad is a tablet computer that, similar to the iPhone, uses a touch screen instead of a stylus or keyboard. It has its own touch screen keyboard and uses a Wi-Fi Internet connection to make it extremely portable. In many ways, it is similar to the iPhone, but larger. It runs the same applications as the iPhone. Jobs admitted Apple had actually

PRODUCT EVENTS

Jobs's announcements of new products for Apple were masterpieces of marketing, and they became media events in themselves. They combined suspense and surprise in a way most people found intriguing. It was said that everyone else tried to avoid making any major announcements on the days when Apple called a press conference or Jobs spoke at a meeting, because whatever Jobs announced was bound to dominate the media that day. Seats at Apple's meetings and announcements were in high demand, and tickets were often rationed. Lines of fans formed outside Apple stores to see the product announcements on video. Internet live blogs of Apple product announcements often attracted larger audiences than regular prime-time television broadcasts. As Moritz said, "Apple announcements were sure to drown out anything emanating from competitors and woe betide the poor politician who had anything to say about the state of the economy on the day that the Cupertino marketing machine . . . broke the sound of silence."[5]

been developing the iPad before the iPhone but had set it aside temporarily to avoid hurting the market for the iPhone.

The iPad was the direct descendant of Apple's Newton MessagePad, developed in 1993. It also showcased Apple's inventiveness, since the device prompted Apple to apply for many patents for technology used in its design.

The iPad was released for purchase in March 2010, and more than 2 million were sold within the first two months, a pace almost double the initial iPhone sales. Writer Stephen Fry, who reviewed the iPad when it was first released, said:

LIBERAL ARTS AND TECHNOLOGY

When Jobs announced the iPad in January 2010, he stood on stage in front of a video display of two street signs. One said "Liberal Arts" and the other said "Technology." Jobs then said, "This is where I have always seen Apple: at the intersection of the liberal arts and technology."[6]

> What [Apple understands] is that if you have an object in your pocket or hand for hours every day, then your relationship with it is profound, human and emotional. Apple's success has been founded on consumer products that address this side of us: their products make users smile as they reach forward to

The iPad announcement was one of many major media events staged by Jobs throughout Apple's history.

manipulate, touch, . . . slide, tweak, pinch, prod, and stroke.[7]

APPLE TV

Apple was not just resting on the success of the iPhone and iPad, however. It had also previously launched Apple TV, a digital media receiver box, in 2007. Designed as an alternative to cable and satellite television services, Apple's Web site described the service:

> *A lot of entertainment. In a very little box. With Apple TV, everything you want to watch —movies, TV shows, photo slideshows, and more—plays wirelessly on your widescreen TV. No managing storage. No syncing to your iTunes library. HD movies and TV shows from iTunes and Netflix play over the Internet on your HDTV, and music and photos stream from your computer. All you have to do is click and watch.*[8]

The receiver was originally going to be called iTV, but because a British company held the rights to the name ITV, Apple renamed its box Apple TV.

PLEASING *STAR TREK* FANS

Some people think the iPad was named in homage to a device in the *Star Trek* television series, the Personal Access Data Device (PADD). The PADD had many of the same features the real iPad does. *Star Trek* fans can now download an app for their iPad that makes it look like the actual PADD used in the *Star Trek: The Next Generation* television series.

iPAD COMPETITION

One of the major competitors for the iPad is the Kindle, marketed by the online bookseller Amazon.com. The Kindle was introduced in 2007 as a way to read books and magazines electronically. It has been upgraded several times and now comes in a color version called the Kindle Fire, introduced in late 2011, that is more like a tablet computer or the iPad, with more expanded features. The Kindle and the iPad dominate the market for e-readers and e-books.

The first version of Apple TV required the user to have a computer running iTunes, and the box was basically designed as an accessory to the computer and iTunes. A major free upgrade in 2008 allowed Apple TV to run as a stand-alone device. Jobs said, "Apple TV was designed to be an accessory for iTunes and your computer. It was not what people wanted. We learned what people wanted was movies, movies, movies."[9]

By the year 2011, Apple was in an enviable position. Not only had it created and successfully marketed devices many consumers could not imagine living without, but it had also managed to create an atmosphere of innovation that set Apple above most other technology companies. But as rumors about Jobs's declining health began circulating, some people began wondering if Apple would be able to continue its winning streak without Jobs and his innovative ideas. +

Jobs discussed his health at a 2008 press conference.
By the end of the decade, it was clear his health was declining.

iCloud

iCloud stores your content and wirelessly pushes it to all your devices.

And because it seamlessly integrates with your apps, everything happens automatically.

Watch the keynote ›

iOS 5
Over 200 new features for iPad, iPhone, and iPod touch.

OS X Lion
The world's most advanced desktop operating system advances even further.

Unveiled in June 2011,
iCloud allows users to access data on multiple devices.

LOOKING TO THE FUTURE

pple was the undisputed leader in portable music with the iPod, as well as in portable computing with the iPad and iPhone and the apps that went with them. It seemed as though the company would continue to come up with innovative ideas, building on its successes as well as exploring new areas of technology. But in January 2011, Jobs announced he would be taking an indefinite medical leave from Apple. He had been diagnosed with pancreatic cancer in 2004 and had undergone surgery and later a liver transplant in 2009. Experts speculated he was dealing with an infection or the rejection of his transplant, or he was taking time to pursue another course of treatment. Investors were nervous, but Apple continued under the direction of Tim Cook, the company's chief operating officer. Jobs stated he would still be involved in the major decisions of the company.

Meanwhile, Apple had surpassed Microsoft in sales and was considered the most valuable consumer brand in the world. The company had come a long way from the Jobs's family garage in California.

NEW PRODUCTS

In 2011, Apple continued refining its existing products, releasing the iPad 2 and the iPhone 4S.

"Thanks to [its] products, Apple has gathered the largest audience ever accumulated by a company that sells anything in a box. Newspapers, magazines, books, movies, albums, board games and videogames—all the things that once required paper, cardboard, plastic, factories, distribution centers, trucking fleets and retail stores—now come in bits on iProducts and can be bought and explored in seconds. Imagine what might lie ahead."[1]

—*Michael Moritz*

> "I believe Apple's brightest and most innovative days are ahead of it. And I look forward to watching and contributing to its success in a new role. I have made some of the best friends of my life at Apple, and I thank you all for the many years of being able to work alongside you."[3]
>
> —*Steve Jobs*
> *in his resignation letter*

Despite his medical leave, Jobs was still seen at the iPad 2 launch in March 2011 and the launch of iCloud in June. iCloud was Apple's new online storage service, which stores and synchronizes music, videos, photos, files, and software for users. Users store content online and then download it to various devices, such as the iPhone or Apple TV. It also serves as a place for users to store Web site bookmarks, calendars, contacts, to-do lists, and other applications so they can use them from any device or computer, and it backs up data to protect it in the event of the loss of a personal device.

In August 2011, Jobs officially resigned from Apple Inc., saying, "I have always said if there ever came a day when I could no longer meet my duties and expectations as Apple's CEO, I would be the first to let you know. Unfortunately, that day has come."[2] Even though most industry experts had foreseen Jobs's resignation, Apple's stock temporarily fell 7 percent.

THE NEXT iPHONE

On October 4, Apple announced the much-anticipated iPhone 4S. It was the most powerful iPhone yet, with a newer, higher-quality camera. It is also the first Apple phone to come equipped with the new Siri feature, a voice-recognition system. Siri was intended to work as a sort of voice-activated personal assistant, according to the Apple Web site:

> *Siri on iPhone 4S lets you use your voice to send messages, schedule meetings, place phone calls, and more. Ask Siri to do things just by talking the way you talk. Siri understands what you say, knows what you mean, and even talks back. Siri is so easy to use and does so much, you'll keep finding more and more ways to use it.*[4]

However, the response to the new iPhone 4S was lukewarm, with many customers feeling the company had not shown any particular innovation. Apple customers with long memories hoped Siri would not repeat the Newton's handwriting recognition failure. Most customers simply felt the phone was not different enough from previous models and determined to wait for an iPhone 5, rumored to debut in 2012.

Just one day after the debut of the iPhone 4S, Apple announced Jobs's death from complications related to his pancreatic cancer. Apple CEO Tim Cook released the following memo to his employees:

> *Team, I have some very sad news to share with all of you. Steve passed away earlier today. Apple has lost a visionary and creative genius, and the world has lost an amazing human being. Those of us who have been fortunate enough to know and work with Steve have lost a dear friend and an inspiring mentor. Steve leaves behind a company that only he could have built, and his spirit will forever be the foundation of Apple. No words can adequately express our sadness at Steve's death or our gratitude for the opportunity to work with him. We will honor his memory by dedicating ourselves to continuing the work he loved so much.*[5]

TRIBUTES

Tributes to Jobs poured in after his death, and they continued to appear online and on a special Apple Web site dedicated to his remembrance. But perhaps one of the most honest assessments came from Jobs himself, in a 2009 interview with Stephen Fry, after Jobs had already experienced several health scares:

> *"Is this then the curtain dropping on your third act?" [Fry asked] "Will you perhaps leave Apple on this high, a fitting end to your career here?"*
>
> *"I don't think of my life as a career," [Jobs said] "I do stuff. I respond to stuff. That's not a career—it's a life!"*[6]

LOOKING FORWARD

Jobs's death left the world wondering if Apple's golden age was over. Skeptics pointed to other companies that had lost their founders and then steadily diminished as a result. However, Apple and its new leader, Tim Cook, continue to look to the future. Jobs was essentially great at coming up with ideas and marketing them, but he also built a team of engineers and experts who could translate those ideas into reality and also generate new ideas themselves.

"There was . . . sweet Steve's capacity for wonderment, the artist's belief in the ideal, the still more beautiful later. Steve's final words, hours earlier, were monosyllables, repeated three times. Before [dying], he'd looked at his sister Patty, then for a long time at his children, then at his life's partner, Laurene, and then over their shoulders past them. Steve's final words were: OH WOW. OH WOW. OH WOW."[7]

—*Mona Simpson describing Jobs's final words in her eulogy*

APPLE'S TRIBUTE

On October 19, 2011, Apple held a tribute to Steve Jobs at its corporate campus in Cupertino, California. Open only to employees, it featured musical performers Norah Jones and Coldplay. All Apple retail stores also closed during the event so employees could watch it on a live video feed. Store windows were covered in white sheets to keep the event private. Another memorial for friends, family, and colleagues was held several days later, featuring people such as Google CEO Larry Page, former US president Bill Clinton, actor Tim Allen, and a performance by U2 lead singer Bono.

Analyst Van Baker commented, "Steve in many ways is still there [be]cause his approach is baked into the Apple culture."[8] Shortly after Jobs's death, there were already rumors of new Apple products debuting in 2012, including the iPhone 5, a touch screen docking iMac, a new version of iTunes on iCloud, an electronic wallet, and an Apple video game console. All of these new products show that Apple is by no means going to wither away with Steve Jobs's death. +

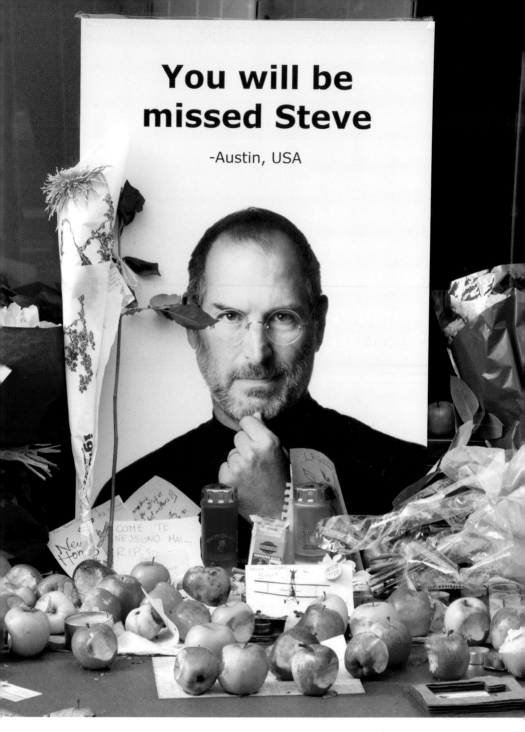

Tributes appeared outside many Apple stores
in the days following Jobs's death.

TIMELINE

1955	1975	1976
Steve Jobs is born in San Francisco, California, on February 24.	Steve Wozniak builds and tests a computer that will become the Apple I.	On April 1, Jobs and Wozniak start the Apple Computer Company.

1983	1984	1985
John Sculley becomes the CEO of Apple in April.	The Macintosh computer is introduced on January 24.	Jobs resigns from Apple on September 17.

1977	1980	1981
The Apple II computer goes on sale in April.	Apple Computer goes public on December 12, making Jobs a millionaire.	Wozniak is involved in a plane crash and takes a leave of absence from Apple.

1986	1996	1997
Jobs starts NeXT in January.	Apple buys NeXT and rehires Jobs.	Jobs becomes Apple's CEO on September 16.

TIMELINE

1998	2001	2003
The iMac is introduced on August 15.	The iPod is introduced on October 23.	The iTunes Store opens on April 28.

2010	2011	2011
The iPad is released in March.	Jobs announces an indefinite leave of absence from Apple in January.	iCloud is introduced in June.

2004

Jobs is diagnosed
with pancreatic
cancer.

2007

Apple Computer
changes its name
to Apple Inc.

2007

Jobs introduces
the iPhone on
January 9.

2011

Jobs resigns
from Apple
in August,
due to poor health.

2011

The iPhone 4S
with Siri
is introduced
on October 4.

2011

Steve Jobs dies on
October 5.

ESSENTIAL FACTS

CREATORS

Steve Wozniak (August 11, 1950–)

Steve Jobs (February 24, 1955–October 5, 2011)

DATE LAUNCHED

April 1, 1976

CHALLENGES

After the success of the Apple I and the Apple II home computers, Apple struggled to remain a viable company, especially after the resignations of both of its founders. After financial failures such as the Apple Lisa and the Newton PDA, it was not until Steve Jobs rejoined the company that it found its niche, both with computers and with other electronic devices.

SUCCESSES

The Apple I was the first truly user-friendly personal computer. The Macintosh computers continue to be very popular, but devices such as the iPhone, iPod, and iPad have made Apple a leader in technology and one of the most popular brand names in the world.

IMPACT ON SOCIETY

Many of Apple's products, including the iPod and the iPhone, have changed the way people all over the world access technology, communicate, and entertain themselves.

QUOTE

"People don't know what they want until you show it to them."

—*Steve Jobs*

GLOSSARY

application
Computer software designed to help the user perform tasks.

browsing
Scanning a text, Web site, or collection of Internet data to gain information.

byte
Eight bits of computer data that together represent a character, number, or color.

calligraphy
Decorative cursive handwriting.

circuit board
A thin, rigid board that contains an electric circuit.

digital
Involving or relating to the use of computer technology.

interface
The point of interaction between computer components, or between the user and the computer.

microchip
A small piece of material that contains many circuits.

microprocessor
A computer processor contained on a chip that interprets computer program instructions and processes data.

MP3
A computer file format for the compression and storage of digital audio data.

port

A physical or virtual connection point on a computer.

programming

A sequence of instructions that enables a computer to do something.

prototype

The original or model on which something is based or formed.

scouts

People who go looking for new ideas and products within their own industry.

software

The programs used to direct the operations of a computer.

tablet

Small rectangular computers that are extremely thin and light.

trackball

A computer pointing device where the user rotates a ball on the surface of a stationary housing.

transistor

A switch in a microchip that controls the output of electricity.

Wi-Fi

An abbreviation for Wireless Fidelity, the wireless networking technology that allows computers and other devices to communicate over a wireless signal.

ADDITIONAL RESOURCES

SELECTED BIBLIOGRAPHY

Isaacson, Walter. *Steve Jobs*. New York: Simon & Schuster, 2011. Print.

Linzmayer, Owen W. *Apple Confidential 2.0*. San Francisco: No Starch, 2008. Print.

Moritz, Michael. *Return to the Little Kingdom: How Apple and Steve Jobs Changed the World*. New York: Overlook, 2010. Print.

Steve Jobs 1955–2011. Spec. issue of *Time*. October 17, 2011. Print.

Young, Jeffrey S., and William L. Simon. *iCon Steve Jobs: The Greatest Second Act in the History of Business*. Hoboken, NJ: John Wiley and Sons, 2005. Print.

FURTHER READINGS

Gillam, Scott. *Steve Jobs: Apple iCon*. Minneapolis, MN: Abdo, 2012. Print.

Goldsworthy, Steve. *Remarkable People: Steve Jobs*. New York: Weigl, 2011.

WEB LINKS

To learn more about Apple, visit ABDO Publishing Company online at **www.abdopublishing.com**. Web sites about Apple are featured on our Book Links page. These links are routinely monitored and updated to provide the most current information available.

PLACES TO VISIT

Apple Store Fifth Avenue
767 Fifth Avenue
New York, NY 10153
212-336-1440
http://www.apple.com/retail/fifthavenue/
The flagship Apple store in New York features a giant glass cube on its plaza.

Computer History Museum
1401 N. Shoreline Boulevard
Mountain View, CA 94043
650-810-1010
http://www.computerhistory.org/
The Computer History Museum is the world's premier museum documenting and exploring the history of computing and its impact on society.

SOURCE NOTES

CHAPTER 1. WHAT YOU NEED BEFORE YOU NEED IT

1. John D. Sutter and Doug Gross. "Apple Unveils the 'Magical' iPad." *CNN Tech*. Cable News Network, 27 Jan. 2010. Web. 10 Nov. 2011.

2. Brad Stone. "Live Blogging the iPad Product Announcement." *New York Times Technology: Bits*. New York Times, 27 Jan. 2010. Web. 10 Nov. 2011.

3. "Steve Jobs Best Quotes Ever." *Wired*. Condé Nast, 29 Mar. 2006. Web. 10 Nov. 2011.

4. Owen W. Linzmayer. *Apple Confidential 2.0*. San Francisco, CA: No Starch Press, 2008. 20.

CHAPTER 2. STEVE JOBS

1. Jeffrey S. Young and William L. Simon. *iCon: Steve Jobs, The Greatest Second Act in the History of Business*. Hoboken, NJ: Wiley, 2005. 134.

2. Ibid. 10.

3. Ibid.

4. Ibid. 15.

CHAPTER 3. THE BIRTH OF APPLE

1. Owen W. Linzmayer. *Apple Confidential 2.0*. San Francisco, CA: No Starch Press, 2008. 3.

2. Michael Moritz. *Return to the Little Kingdom: How Apple and Steve Jobs Changed the World*. New York: Overlook, 2009. 110.

3. Steve Wozniak and Gina Smith. *iWoz: Computer Geek to Cult Icon: How I Invented the Personal Computer, Co-Founded Apple, and Had Fun Doing It*. New York: Norton, 2007. 166.

4. Owen W. Linzmayer. *Apple Confidential 2.0*. San Francisco, CA: No Starch Press, 2008. 5.

5. Ibid. 6.

6. Michael Moritz. *Return to the Little Kingdom: How Apple and Steve Jobs Changed the World*. New York: Overlook, 2009. 150–151.

7. Owen W. Linzmayer. *Apple Confidential 2.0.* San Francisco, CA: No Starch Press, 2008. 9.

CHAPTER 4. FROM THE GARAGE TO THE WORLD

1. Owen W. Linzmayer. *Apple Confidential 2.0.* San Francisco, CA: No Starch Press, 2008. 12.

2. Michael Moritz. *Return to the Little Kingdom: How Apple and Steve Jobs Changed the World.* New York: Overlook, 2009. 250.

CHAPTER 5. GROWING PAINS

1. Owen W. Linzmayer. *Apple Confidential 2.0.* San Francisco, CA: No Starch Press, 2008. 67.

2. Ibid. 82.

3. Ibid. 92.

4. Ibid. 117.

5. Ibid. 96.

6. Jeffrey S. Young and William L. Simon. *iCon: Steve Jobs, The Greatest Second Act in the History of Business.* Hoboken, NJ: Wiley, 2005. 98.

7. Ibid. 97.

8. Owen W. Linzmayer. *Apple Confidential 2.0.* San Francisco, CA: No Starch Press, 2008. 157.

CHAPTER 6. APPLE'S NeXT STEP

1. Jeff Goodell, "Steve Jobs in 1994: The Rolling Stone Interview." *Rolling Stone.* Rolling Stone, 17 Jan. 2011. Web. 10 Nov. 2011.

2. Owen W. Linzmayer. *Apple Confidential 2.0.* San Francisco, CA: No Starch Press, 2008. 200.

3. Ibid. 203.

4. John Markoff. "Former Chief Executive Offers Apple Encouragement and Says Old Strategy Can Still Work." *New York Times.* New York Times, 13 May 1996. Web. 10 Nov. 2011.

SOURCE NOTES CONTINUED

CHAPTER 7. BACK TO APPLE

1. Michael Moritz. *Return to the Little Kingdom: How Apple and Steve Jobs Changed the World.* New York: Overlook, 2009. 335.

2. Ibid. 335.

3. "The Stores." *ifoAppleStore.com.* ifoAppleStore, n.d. Web. 10 Nov. 2011.

4. Ibid.

CHAPTER 8. THE AGE OF iTUNES

1. Jennifer Bergen. "Apple iPod: The First Ten Years." *PCMag.com.* Ziff Davis, 23 Oct. 2011. Web. 10 Nov. 2011.

2. Jeffrey S. Young and William L. Simon. *iCon: Steve Jobs, The Greatest Second Act in the History of Business.* Hoboken, NJ: Wiley, 2005. 274.

3. Ibid. 284.

4. Ibid.

5. "Newsweek Interview: Steve Jobs, Apple CEO." *PR Newswire.* PR Newswire, 15 Oct. 2006. Web. 10 Nov. 2011.

CHAPTER 9. IN THE PALM OF YOUR HAND

1. Michael Moritz. *Return to the Little Kingdom: How Apple and Steve Jobs Changed the World.* New York: Overlook, 2009. 340.

2. "The Apple of Your Ear." *Time.* Time, 12 Jan. 2007. Web. 10 Nov. 2011.

3. Ryan Block, "Live from Macworld 2007: Steve Jobs' Keynote Address." Engadget, January 9, 2007. Web. http://www.engadget.com/2007/01/09/live-from-macworld-2007-steve-jobs-keynote/

4. Steven Fry. "The iPad Launch: Can Steve Jobs Do It Again?" *Time.* Time, 1 Apr. 2010. Web. 10 Nov. 2011.

5. Michael Moritz. *Return to the Little Kingdom: How Apple and Steve Jobs Changed the World.* New York: Overlook, 2009. 339.

6. Steven Fry. "The iPad Launch: Can Steve Jobs Do It Again?" *Time*. Time, 1 Apr. 2010. Web. 10 Nov. 2011.

7. Ibid.

8. "Apple TV." *Apple*. Apple Company, n.d. Web. 10 Nov. 2011.

9. Cliff Edwards. "Jobs Appeal to the Crowd." *Bloomberg Businessweek*. Bloomberg, 15 Jan. 2008. Web. 10 Nov. 2011.

CHAPTER 10. LOOKING TO THE FUTURE

1. Michael Moritz. *Return to the Little Kingdom: How Apple and Steve Jobs Changed the World.* New York: Overlook, 2009. 341.

2. Poornima Gupta. "Steve Jobs resigns from Apple, Cook becomes CEO." *Reuters*. Thomson Reuters, 24 Aug. 2011. Web. 10 Nov. 2011.

3. "Text: Letter from Steve Jobs resigning as Apple CEO." *Reuters*. Thomson Reuters, 24 Aug. 2011. Web. 10 Nov. 2011.

4. "iPhone: Siri." *Apple*. Apple Company, n.d. Web. 10 Nov. 2011.

5. E. B. Boyd, "Apple's Official Announcement on the Death of Steve Jobs." *Fast Company*. Fast Company, 5 Oct. 2011. Web. 10 Nov. 2011.

6. Steven Fry. "The iPad Launch: Can Steve Jobs Do It Again?" *Time*. Time, 1 Apr. 2010. Web. 10 Nov. 2011.

7. Mona Simpson. "A Sister's Eulogy for Steve Jobs." *New York Times*. New York Times, 30 Oct. 2011. Web. 10 Nov. 2011.

8. Scott Martin and Jon Swartz. "Apple's Future Looks Secure." *USA Today*. USA Today, 6 Oct. 2011. Web. 10 Nov. 2011.

INDEX

ABOUT THE AUTHOR

Marcia Amidon Lusted is the author of more than 60 books for young readers as well as hundreds of magazine articles. She is an assistant editor for Cobblestone Publishing, a writing instructor, and a musician. She lives in New Hampshire with her family.

PHOTO CREDITS